Let us make a white winter out of the "dark winter",

let us illuminate the darkness!

Overcoming Fear

Exercises for spiritual self-defense

by Thomas Mayer

Dear Readers,

the reason for this book on overcoming fear is the corona crisis that began in 2020. This brought to the surface unresolved issues that will occupy us for a long time. The exercises presented in this book are timeless and can be used for other occasions as well – for example, wars, social crises, conflicts and pressures of all kinds.

In this little book, I present 28 meditations and soul-exercises that aim to strengthen our sovereignty, dignity and connection to the spirit; this should contribute to ease the shared situation.

In Latin, corona means "crown" and "corona radiata" means "halo". The crown is an expression of an upright and awakened crown chakra that connects us with the spiritual world; a particularly strong connection is expressed through the halo.

The corona crisis at its core is an attack on mankind's connection to spirituality. Since it is a spiritual war, it can only be met with spiritual means.

The suggestions made in this booklet are not designed only for reading, but also for meditating. It is best to do this in small groups and to then discuss the experiences.

"Dark winter" is the name given to an international conference in 2001 in which lockdowns were played out. Let us make a white winter out of it, let us illuminate the darkness! I chose this as the concept for the pictures in this booklet.

Since my youth I have been practicing anthroposophy; today I mainly give courses and trainings in anthroposophical meditation. Parallel to this I have always engaged as a civil rights activist, working for more direct democracy and for a fair money system. It is from this background that I wrote this text.

I wish you pleasure in reading, meditating and talking about it!

March, 2023

Thomas Mayer

Contents

Spiritual scientific perspective on the corona crisis

Introduction

The lockdowns of the corona crisis since March 2020 present a spiritual challenge. I perceive these as a worldwide attack on human consciousness. It is an attempt to bind people to fear and cut them off from their sovereign core. It is a huge challenge.

Throughout this it is important to stay aware and to strengthen your sovereignty and your connection to spirituality. With that aim I present the following 28 Meditations and Soul-exercises. Through these we are able to act and are not powerless, it only depends on us. We are sovereign. This strengthens our dignity.

The lockdowns from March 2020 onwards surprisingly revealed what suddenly was possible, or what was no longer possible – restriction of fundamental rights, defamation of people and scientists with sober arguments, one-sided information by the media. No doubt the corona infection was a severe disease, like any other infection. But why did it generate so much fear? And why this massive violation of the foundations of our society? Lockdown is a term used in the penal system; it means "locking the prison cell". Whole countries were locked up. The feeling grew that we were living in a George Orwell novel. After a short period of relaxation in the summer of 2020 the governments decided to continue with devastating lockdowns lasting for months. The damages far outweighed the benefits. Worldwide far more people were going to die due to the results of the lockdowns than through the illness itself, but there was no open discussion about this proportionality. Instead, pressure was built up for people to be vaccinated, thus dividing the population.[1]

Many of us could sense how something was being thrust upon us with an immense force, something not aiming at freedom or love. A tremendous, dark, overpowering something was lingering over our life and society. This caused fear.

An antidote to this is self-reflection and meditation. This strengthens our individual power and creates freedom. And by spiritual and healing deeds we can drain the spiritual energy out of the attacks, thereby easing the collective thinking and feeling. This helps social development. Inner and outer actions belong together.

To me, it is important to never lose love or our spiritual connection. The danger is to become embittered through criticizing the measures of the state and thus giving room precisely to the dark forces one is afraid of.

The 28 meditations presented here have proven helpful. It is best to practice them together with others and then to share the experiences. This sharing of experiences is essential in order to digest them. If you are just by yourself, it is recommended you write down your experiences. There is no need to do the exercises in a certain order; you can choose the exercise you find suitable. If you cannot relate to an exercise, just leave it.

The following meditations are intended to address those with a spiritual interest, no matter what spiritual background they are from. I have done my best to be understandable. The following is not meant for those convinced that there is only a material world, as they will not understand. For me the soul-world and the spiritual

world are a daily experienced reality. This is the starting point for the following exercises.

For almost 20 years I have taught anthroposophical meditation. Anthroposophy is the science of the spiritual world. Many things here I can only describe aphoristically. The practice of meditation and the exploration of the spiritual world is a huge and complex field. At the end of this text, I have gathered together spiritual-scientific perspectives on the corona crisis. Many questions will remain open. This is good, because it is stimulating.

The worldwide lockdowns since March 2020 were unimaginable to us citizens. But they were already planned and played through in several international conferences, e.g. "Dark winter" in 2001. The term "dark winter" or "hard winter" was repeatedly chosen by politicians in 2020/21.[2] Spiritually we can turn it into a white winter. The photographs in this booklet are meant to encourage this.

Basic meditations

Exercise 1:

**Create moments free of fear and strengthen
your connection to spirituality**

The corona restrictions left a big mark on our daily lives
– the fear of becoming ill, the fear of the consequences of
the restrictions and the continuous media bombardment
exposed many of us to a permanent gruelling corona
stress. We need corona-free moments every day in which
we can let ourselves be filled with something nourishing
such as a walk in the woods, a good book, good conversations, pleasant experiences or a meditation. Medita-

tion is always about strengthening the connection to the spirit. Here is a simple example:

Exercise: I put myself into a relaxed and upright sitting position, focus my attention on myself and become aware of myself. How do I feel in my body, what mood do I carry in my heart, what's happening in my thoughts? After a while of becoming self-aware, I dwell on the sentence "Christ in me" – (or "Buddha in me"; depending on whom I feel connected to.) Stay with "Christ in me" and create an inner space, so that the warming love of Christ – or the sublime serenity of Buddha – can penetrate your soul and body. Restlessness and tension may appear during the process, but that is OK. Just stay with Christ, or Buddha, for five minutes or more.

Exercise 2:

Do many small meditations and prayers throughout the day

Botho Sigwart zu Eulenburg was a gifted composer who died in 1915 during the First World War at the age of 31. His sisters and cousins stayed in regular inner contact with him and for decades they wrote down what he told them. His very intimate and touching messages are published in two volumes entitled *The Bridge over the River* (Anthroposophic Press 1974). Sigwart described in detail his experiences after death and how he accompanied his friends throughout the pitch-black times of World War I and II. Over and over again he described the brightness and purity of the higher regions of the spiritual world, while masses of dark demons were raging on earth and in the lower astral regions, infiltrating into people's thoughts and feelings. He constantly encouraged us to seek the connection to the spirit. Yet, in such dark days, it is not enough to meditate or pray only twice or three times daily. Because of the massive number of demons, the time gaps through which they can enter are too long. This is why Sigwart recommended praying preferably once every hour or to meditate or create a little contemplative space. Only in so doing do we create a spiritual rampart, closed in such a way that the demons can no longer invade.

Exercise: Speak your prayer every hour or linger meditatively with a strengthening thought. Ask yourself every hour: Am I in a good condition; am I connected to the right kind of spirits?

Clarifying your emotional space

Exercise 3:

Turning rage and anger into strength and clarity

Thinking about the lockdowns is a big emotional challenge for me. I envision the following situation:

- The lockdowns since March 2020 have caused devastating damage to our physical and mental health, to the economy, public finances, democracy, social trust, and so on.

- It is already certain by now that many more people are likely to die from the restrictions than from the virus infection itself. Presumably, this is also the case for Germany, but definitely for Third World countries, where millions of people will starve to death.

- Many investigations show that lockdowns are useless. They hardly bring help against the virus, in contrast to focused help for groups at high risk and voluntary measures.[3]

- All this does not really interest our politicians and the media as they have long since abandoned evidence-based politics. The lockdowns are a political decision, as the now ex-German chancellor, Angela Merkel, emphasized.

- It is all so terrible that I can hardly bear it.

The more I reflect on the above, the more disappointment, anger and rage accumulate in me. I know that I am not alone in this. What is to be done? Through getting angry I am hurting myself, I feel miserable and robbed of my energy. Nevertheless, you can turn it into something productive, as there is also always positive will-power lying within the anger.

Exercise: I stand up. Anger rises up within me; I experience it, I feel and welcome it. Now I direct the anger through my body, my legs and my feet down into the ground. Anger leaves me, setting free the will-power lying within, which now rises up and fills me. I experience my will-power and give it room. In my limbs I feel strength, my head becomes clearer. This will-power I can use later for action, but for now it is a matter of permeating myself with it, accumulating it within myself. I increasingly resemble an oak tree. How do I feel now, is my anger still present?

Exercise 4:

Sort, clarify and observe emotions

The transformation of anger, as proposed, usually only works partially, as soul-life is complex. The corona lockdowns have provoked many feelings in all of us.

The media and the government systematically generated tremendous fear of the corona virus in society which brought hidden fears in people to the surface, such as the fear of death, fear of losing livelihood, fear of exclusion, all fears that have long been slumbering in our souls. A kind of extensive re-traumatizing took place, but the fears were projected onto the virus. This explains the enormous agitation that the virus alone would not have been able to produce. The problem with this is that hidden fears come up which can be felt by our soul, but there is no process of integration because these fears are projected onto the virus and thus detached from their original context. The actual issues are obfuscated and not seen.

The same mechanism can also take place if, for example, one is afraid of a health dictatorship. It is possible, for instance, that unresolved traumas with an authoritarian father or other traumatizing experiences are triggered.

Herein lies a great opportunity. Through the lockdowns we get in touch with our soul shadows and now have the chance to illuminate and integrate them.

Exercise: I collect and note down my feelings caused by the lockdowns. I try to specify every single feeling by asking questions. How do I sense it in my body, e.g. tightness, pressure, tension, and so on? What kind of emotion is it, rage, despair, fear, helplessness, and so on? What particular qualities or colourings does it have? To what does the feeling refer? For instance, if I am afraid, am I afraid of illness, political oppression or economic extermination? And with every single emotion, I ask myself, is a personal theme being triggered or am I participating in the collective mood? I note down my feelings, appreciate them, perceive them and dwell in them. It is important and healing to dwell in your feelings before you do something else with them.

Exercise 5:

Healing power over dark feelings

While sorting your feelings, some will stand out and require help and redemption. Such inner work is often a long process. The following is a basic exercise.

Exercise: I sense a feeling of distress and look at it from an observer perspective, for example, from the standpoint of my personal angel. I ask myself, what does this feeling need, which so far I have not given it? Then, I do something good for this stressful emotion and pray into it, for example, the Lord's Prayer or another kind of prayer. Or I offer it a beautiful tune or melody by singing into it. Finally, I look at the feeling again. Has it changed? Does it need something else?

Light up your thinking space

Exercise 6:

Strengthen independent thinking and believe your own insights

As contemporaries, we find ourselves constantly bombarded by the media with information, the sheer amount of which overwhelms us and thus often sinks into us unprocessed. This befogs and darkens our thinking space.

By contrast, independent thinking and acquiring your own insights are a significant spiritual deed. If you pay attention, you will notice how your own consciousness changes and becomes light-filled through this. When I myself think thoughts that are logical and clear, I perceive this as an inner sunrise in a crystal-clear mountain landscape; everything becomes bright, light and clear. For in thinking we are already in the spiritual world. Through independent thinking we invite corresponding spirits of light, who then fill our conscious space. Thomas Aquinas, the great scholastic of the Middle Ages, spoke of thought needing to be christianized. He still knew that thinking is always also communication with spiritual beings.

I now would like to present a simple thought-exercise on the corona issue.

Every year, about 950,000 people die in Germany. The average life expectancy in Germany is 81 years. These figures are supplied by the Federal Office of Statistics (Statistisches Bundesamt). Women on average live longer (83.4 years), men die somewhat sooner (78.6 years); 81 years is the average value.[5]

What does the figure 81 mean? It means that life ends with death; there is no eternal life possible in the physical body. At some point this body gets too rickety and "gives up its spirit", as the saying goes. This means the spirit departs. Thirty years ago, life expectancy was about 10 years less. Due mainly to medical progress, people today live longer.

Two more figures: In 2020, according to the figures of the state-run RKI in Germany, a total of 33,960 people died with a positive corona test,[6] that is, 3.6 percent of the total of 950,000 deaths. The actual cause of death, whether with or from the corona-virus, are not taken into account here, even if the infection in most cases was only the last drop that caused the barrel of the pre-existing illnesses to overflow. 3.6 percent tested positive, whereas 96.4 percent died without a positive test from cardiovascular diseases, cancer, lung inflammation, other infections and countless other illnesses. In comparison to 96.4 percent, 3.6 percent is quite small. 3.6 percent indicates that covid19 is a comparatively insignificant cause of death. Most other causes of death are more significant.

The RKI published the result that the average age of those who died with positive tests was 84 years old (as of January 2021).[7] 84 is three years older than normal life expectancy. This means that, on average, people die about three years earlier from the well-known diseases than from covid19. Thus, the coronavirus does not increase the average mortality and it is not more dangerous than the rest of life.

At this point, it is good to pause. On the basis of the available figures, do these considerations and classifications make logical sense? Can I think them myself? If so, do I have a sense of truth in the conclusion that the coronavirus is not more dangerous than the rest of life? If I perceive this as being true, do I then also believe it? If I linger in the feeling of truth, what does this stir up in me? How do I now perceive my consciousness, what quality do I perceive now?

It could be that immediately resistance to this insight comes up and wipes away the sense of truth. "It cannot be that the coronavirus is no more dangerous than the rest of life, because otherwise this indeed contradicts everything that our governments and mainstream media have been telling us on a daily basis." Connected with such thoughts fear can arise in the soul that you stand alone or are cast out.

Such resistance must be respected. From where does it originate? In any case, it has nothing to do with the insight that 84 is more than 81.

One can think further about the figures. In 2020, we experienced two lockdowns. Does this change the picture? In thought, one can see at least three possibilities: Without lockdowns, would so many more people have died with covid19 and at an earlier age so that it would have become a more significant illness? Or did the lockdowns make no significant difference compared with what purposeful, voluntary protective measures would have done? Or did the lockdowns, through the collateral damage, even lead to a higher mortality?

In order to work further on these questions in a serious way, it is necessary to look at empirical studies.

Exercise: I think through the given figures and their significance and talk to others about this. In doing so, I pause ever again and observe what is happening in my soul.

Exercise 7:

Search for truth and go to the sources

The constant search for truth is a central spiritual and, of course, also a scientific state of mind. This is nothing abstract, but rather a longing to connect with higher, light-filled spiritual beings. "I am the way, the truth and the life." We can take these words of Christ at face value – the search for truth, spiritually speaking, is the christianisation of thinking. To feel the presence of Christ, of angels or other sublime spirits in one's own thinking is one of the most significant experiences of consciousness one can have.

You should never give up the search for truth and never blindly trust. This has always been the case, but is even more important today. It is easy to manipulate in today's media world; one only needs to inform one-sidedly and conceal contradictory facts. That is why we should also always look at the sources. In the corona crisis, this was a shocking exercise for me. Let me give you an example.

How does one get to the sources? Thanks to the internet, there are many possibilities today. The blogs of various scientific journalists helped me with their discussions of diverse scientific studies, always including links so that the original texts could easily be accessed.

Example: "asymptomatically-infected" people

Until 2019, the position of mainstream medicine was that people suffering from viral infections could be contagious, but healthy people could not be. In the case of infections, viruses multiply on a large scale in the cells of the body, then the immune system reacts to it and you develop a cough, catch a fever or suffer from aching limbs. Without symptoms of a disease, there is no particular virus multiplication and consequently no virusload to pass on. The days before the symptoms appear, while the viruses are already multiplying, you can possibly be contagious. This is called "pre-symptomatic contagion". This was state of the art science until 2019.

But then came the corona-virus and everything was different. Suddenly there were also "asymptomatic diseased" people who were said to be contagious and should be feared. People who were called "healthy" before the end of 2019 were now being designated as "asymptomatically ill". Due to this theory something was turned upside down – not the sick, but the healthy had to go into quarantine. For the first time in world-history, a worldwide lockdown was imposed on everybody, since those "asymptomatically diseased" could infect others. Since one could not see who is "asymptomatically ill", because there were no symptoms, everyone had to be isolated. This was the reasoning, too, behind making masks compulsory.

What is most remarkable is that even one year after the lockdown, there is still no scientific proof at all that "asymptomatically diseased people" are contagious. There are many studies in which the contacts of individual corona-positive people without symptoms were carefully checked. No infections were found in their vicinity. There is even a study of all 10 million inhabitants of Wuhan, an incredibly large study that found as good as no contagion by asymptomatically diseased people.[8]

The first "asymptomatic contagious case" in Germany, a Chinese lady on her business trip in January 2020, which Herr Drosten published in a widely read scientific article, turned out, after all, to not be a case, since the Chinese woman did have symptoms and had taken medication to reduce her fever. Further studies claiming that asymptomatic contagion exists never provided proof through actual case studies. They can also not explain how the contagion could work, as with the non-existence of the illness no high viral-load is present. These studies argue instead that it is often unclear with many infections how the contagion took place. It is then concluded that the diseased must have gotten infected by asymptomatically ill people. But this is only an assumption and not proof. It was also confirmed by the WHO that there was no evidence of asymptomatic contagion. Moreover, according to the German RKI: "These contagions, however, likely play a subordinate role." Because of the unproven theory of "asymptomatic contagion" nearly the whole world was sent into a lockdown. Phew, this makes you take a deep breath!

At this point a fundamental problem of modern science becomes evident. Many scientists are seeking the truth; they are therefore interested in phenomena and perception and also regard science as being ethically sound.

However, there is a growing number of scientists who mainly sit in front of the computer and create models. These models and extrapolations usually have false basic assumptions and thus produce incorrect results; but this is not so important as the model replaces perception. It is then no longer important that one cannot find asymptomatic contagion in actual, concrete investigations. One does not even need confirmation in perception at all; the model itself is sufficient enough for confirmation.

And the fact that fear-mongering arguments are delivered in order to paralyse entire countries through lockdowns

– not even this produces a bad conscience. We are dealing here with detached "science", detached from the real world and detached from moral conscience. Of course, you have to ask yourself, what kind of spirits are at work here?

How else could the unknown paths of contagion be explained? The trivial concept of getting hit by a virus similar to a bullet does not correspond to reality. A virus alone has no impact and viruses are everywhere. This is well known in mainstream medicine. Up to 95 percent of all people, for example, carry in their bodies the Epstein-Barr virus, but hardly anyone suffers from Pfeiffer's disease (mononucleosis). Thus the virus alone does not cause the disease. It is always necessary to have an openness or a weak immune system for an infectious disease to occur. A weakening of the immune system can

be caused by biographical, psychic or mental tensions or crises. It is known that anxiety and powerlessness weaken the immune system, making you more susceptible to disease. In order to comprehend the covid19 disease where there were no clear contagion paths, people would have to be examined according to their susceptibility. It is very likely that the fomented corona panic and the lockdown stress was a major cause of many covid19 illnesses. This could also be examined through broad-scale psychological studies, but such studies are not undertaken.

The study of the sources is sobering. With regard to corona, there are a lot of contradictions between the results of proper research and the opinions published in the media. Another example: Since January 2021, the lockdowns have been justified by virus mutations, said to be more contagious and more dangerous. All that is based on man-made models. But reality is different. The result of 1.5 million tests in England showed that these mutations are about six percent more contagious, which hardly makes any difference. The number of hospitalizations and deaths went down in Ireland, England and South Africa, as in other countries, despite the mutations.[9] Why are the modellers and our governments not interested that reality is so different from their computer calculations?

I learned to appreciate the genuine and open science that seeks for truth and relies on perceptible reality. Here the spirit of Christ is active.

Exercise: Believe nothing, not even me, but always remain critical and unbiased. Make it a habit of always going to the sources and examining them. This clarifies your thinking.

Exercise 8:

Dealing with the corona crisis in a positive way

Our politicians confronted us with constantly changing, complicated restrictions that became ever more nonsensical. This confused people and many conversations about this took place. The problem is, by getting upset about the restrictions you fettered your own emotional energy and that fed the field of collective fear and compulsion.

A good possibility to get beyond this negative spiral is never to remain with a negative thought, but always to be awake in your thinking and weigh up in your soul what positive possibilities exist. It is not about whether these possibilities can be put into practice, but about strengthening your own soul and leaving an imprint on the collective mental environment. Imagine millions of people repeatedly thinking positive alternatives – what a force this would be! Of course, we can only begin with ourselves by taking on the responsibility for our own thinking.

Exercise: Think positive alternatives to lockdowns and regulations and observe what happens in your soul. With negative descriptions of circumstances the energy and mood sinks; with positive thoughts the energy and mood should rise again. Some examples:

– During lockdown, sport was forbidden, everyone was supposed to stay at home and, through this, immune systems were weakened.

Positive thinking: A state-run advertising agency campaigns for a daily one-hour walk in nature. Everyone is to go out and exercise. In the towns, free shuttle busses are provided to drive you to local recreation areas.

– Today, a high number of infections is seen as terrible and threatening.

Positive thinking: A high number of infections is normal and good in the flu season, since through this the immunity in the population is increased.

– Lockdowns since 2020 were justified by the threat of overcrowding of hospitals. In actual fact, in 2020 during the corona pandemic, 20 hospitals with 2,100 beds were closed and more than 4,000 emergency beds were shut down in Germany, for which politicians were responsible.

Positive thinking: hospitals receive more funding so that they can survive. The nursing profession is made more attractive by increasing wages for care professionals in order to end the care crisis in hospitals and homes for the elderly.

– And so on.

How to avoid the corona hypnosis caused by media consumption

The continuous shower of messages, often received in a half-sleepy consciousness through radio, television and smart phone, is like a hypnosis. When, for example, you hear twenty times a day that the corona virus is very dangerous, at some point you believe it. This is how belief systems are anchored in.

Opinion surveys showed that people overestimated the danger of the corona virus about 300-600 times. Not double or ten times but 600 times.[10] How is this possible?

A psychologist who works with hypnosis therapy wrote in a newsletter: "The news reports on covid19 fulfill, since March 2020, all the criteria for a mass hypnosis." Since it makes more understandable what happened since March 2020, I will quote in more detail:

"Hypnosis is a trance induced from without. Trance means a condition of focussed attention – the attention is only focussed on one theme or chosen aspects of that theme. At the same time your own control mechanisms are shut down; what is said no longer has to be logical in order to be accepted. Your understanding no longer gauges the situation. It is not possible to put things in perspective anymore; we no longer ask, 'Is this really true? Or could one view it differently?'

In psychotherapy this helps to look beyond one's own horizon and to find new solutions. But pathological or unhealthy trances exist, where we end up with narrow tunnel vision. This is currently happening to many people quite involuntarily and without their noticing it!

The most common techniques of the language of hypnosis are:

- the continuous repetition of contents or certain words that are supposed to make an impact.

- the activating of as many senses as possible (the touching of a door handle – feeling). 'Is corona transmitted through food?' (taste). Pictures of bottles of disinfection (smell). Reports from the emergency ward (seeing and hearing).

- emotionally loaded words (crisis, quarantine, unpredictable, increase, casualties, killer virus, invisible danger, pandemic, spreading, shocking, in tears, ...).

- constant new details, so that one is no longer able to think straight.

- above all, contradictions. Hypnosis works intentionally with contradictions, because contradictions lead to confusion – and in a condition of confusion, people can be maximally influenced and are ready to trust a real or imagined authority. Precisely this can be observed everywhere at present.

If someone finds themselves in a corona-hypnosis, you notice the following phenomena:

- It is no longer possible to keep a distance from the theme and think objectively about it.

- Emotions such as fear or insecurity as well as helplessness dominate.

- Continuously new information is sought; the theme is daily centre stage and each detail confirms your previous opinion.

In order not to succumb to this corona-hypnosis it is recommendable:

- To get an information update once or twice a day and to then put aside your phone.

- To minimize the arbitrary consumption of media, for example, through the car radio, also of social media. Rather search for information in a targeted manner.

- To become aware of what gives us strength and what brings us into contact with the here and now. To replenish the sources of strength in order to remain able to do things, for example, in nature, with friends or in the family or with our favourite music.

- To connect to people who support us in our endeavours, putting ourselves forward for that which is our heart's concern even if it is difficult and demands courage.

- To abstain from complaining and bewailing. Not to focus on what is terrible, but on what we concretely can and have to do – regardless of whether we are sure of our success, whether we have a short distance to go or rather have to run a marathon."

What, however, do we do with others suffering from corona-hypnosis? Here the psychologist writes: "Unfortunately, it is not possible to convince through logical arguments people in our surrounding who have succumbed to the language of hypnosis. This is exactly what is no longer possible. But we can convince through emotions and our own example – to mention, by the way, that we are not worried about corona (this produces confusion, since it does not fit with what is permanently being communicated and consequently also has a hypnotic effect), by keeping our humour, staying friendly, asking a friend quite naturally whether we might hug them, giving others security and helping them. Radiate confidence. Whoever acts positively is convincing, whoever emits what people long for in their need, is also better equipped to convince.

The de-hypnotizing takes place mostly through the back door, unnoticed, in the same way as the hypnosis."

Let us therefore begin with ourselves. All previous meditations and soul-exercises already worked in the direction of de-hypnosis. Let us now concern ourselves with our own media consumption.

Exercise: Avoid unconscious media consumption. Simply turn off the radio or television when you do something else. Limit media consumption to a short time, inform yourself consciously and always actively process the information. Is it logical? Does this fit in with my previous knowledge? What intention does the author have? What does it mean? Meet all media information with the processing activity of your consciousness. Best to take in very little, but in the right way.

Clarifying my position in society

Exercise 10:

Meditate different points of view, create space for understanding

The points of view concerning lockdowns in society are very disparate; open conversations seldom occur. Denying a conversation is a form of wielding power and should in no case be adopted, but consciously dismantled. For this the following exercise should serve. The result should never be influenced by a previously existing inner sympathy or antipathy. This exercise is not about right or wrong but about taking on different standpoints.

Exercise: In the first part of the exercise, in quiet contemplation, carefully imagine yourself in the lockdown situation here in Germany and other neighbouring countries. Imagine or cultivate in yourself the feeling that the lockdowns, the governmental restrictions with mask mandates, social distancing, travel restrictions, and so on, were made with the best of intentions to protect the individual person. Cultivate in yourself the feeling of being well cared for and protected by the government and completely trust the inflicted mandates in quiet confidence. Everything is good and necessary and after the crisis everything will return to its stable and secure everyday pattern. This picture should be carefully held within and receive adequate emotional space.

In the second part of the exercise, you again build up a comprehensive picture of the lockdowns and restrictions. But now you put the situation into question. Carefully test the claims of various positions and study the different points of view of the experts; observe the event comprehensively. Now witness that the relationship between the apparent danger of the virus and the measures taken is indeed in the greatest measure grotesquely out of proportion. Experience the taken measures and the apparent danger of the virus as a deeply suggestive event, equal to a lie, but purporting to be the ethically totally correct stance and only possible path.

With this exercise it is important to distance yourself from your already existing inner position and to create an openness. How do these two polar pictures and basic moods work back on the soul; what takes place in your innermost being?

Exercise 11:

What is the higher meaning of the corona crisis?

Many people wondered why the spiritual world allowed the lockdowns. Have the good gods left us for the time being? Is this the beginning of a dark age of soulless materialism and state surveillance, replacing the brief historical dawn of the age of enlightenment, human rights and freedom? Or is there a higher meaning in the corona crisis? Is it meant to stimulate inner processes of growth? Are old shadows to be brought to the surface in order to be faced? There are no quick and easy answers to these questions. It is important to get into an open, seeking mode.

Exercise: Meditate on the question: "What is the higher meaning of the corona crisis?" In order to get a broader perspective, connect yourself with special places in nature or with sublime spiritual beings and reflect upon this question together with them.

Exercise 12:

Reconsidering your own position in society

For many people the lockdowns caused a fundamental shock to their social framework. It is essential to come to terms with this, to feel through this in order to re-position yourself.

Exercise: Think and feel through the following questions:

- Who constitutes my supportive community?

- Do I trust the state? Has anything changed here?

- Am I ready to stand for democracy, freedom of speech and fundamental rights? Am I prepared to allow these values to shine forth regardless of how many of these values are present in society?

- Which media do I want to support by way of subscriptions or to give my attention to?

- What aspects of a political party are important that it become acceptable for me?

- What impact does the new risk factor of lockdowns have on my economic activities? At the beginning of 2020 lockdowns were unthinkable. Now we are threatened by a constant repetition, as new viruses and new mutations arise every year. How can I financially protect myself against this new danger?

- And so on.

Exercise 13:

Enduring insult and denial

If one proceeds thoroughly, one notices in the official corona politics many things which do not make sense. Critical public discussion since March 2020, however, almost only took place in alternative media and small scientific blogs. If people expressed critical views in public and questioned the adequacy of the restrictions and limitations of basic rights, they were exposed to hate and marginalization. The driving forces for this were the government and the mainstream media. To show you what I mean, I will give an example.

On 29 August 2020 a large alternative demonstration took place with 100,000-120,000 people in Tiergarten – the central public park in Berlin. The key speakers were reputable; they criticized the corona measures as being incompatible with our basic rights and demanded adherence to these. The participants were a cross-section of society – there were many academics, many self-employed people, many supporters of the Green Party and the SPD (Germany's Social Democrats). The demonstration reminded one of the peace movement and the environmental awareness movement at the inception of the Green Party. Everything was peaceful. This comes across clearly in the videos of the demonstration.

This demonstration was initially forbidden by the Berlin Minister for the Interior, Andreas Geisel, the reason being that he did not want to give a stage to rightwing extremists and conspiracy theorists. This ban was overturned in court.

On 29 August 2020 in Berlin there were other smaller demonstrations that were not forbidden by the Minister of the Interior, amongst them a demonstration directly in front of the Berlin Reichstag (the parliament building), organized by Rüdiger Hoffmann. Hoffmann is considered a rightwing extremist and was sentenced for attempted murder. He had organized an attack on a home for refugees with Molotov-cocktail bombs. Since 2013 Hoffmann had organized an annual "storming of the Reichstag".[11] His demonstration in August 2020 in the no-protest zone in front of the Reichstag was permitted by the Minister of the Interior. This was contrary to the law, since for this the Minister would have had to seek permission from the Federal Ministry of the Interior, which he did not do, as later came out. Only three policemen guarded the steps to the Reichstag. This is the

background to the "storming of the Reichstag"; in actual fact it was a photo opportunity on the steps of the Reichstag. Nobody actually entered the Reichstag.

With this the framing was complete, the media only reported on the "storming of the Reichstag"; all government parties outdid each other in taking offence; special honouring was given to the three courageous policemen in parliament. Nothing was reported in the media about the huge peaceful demonstration for the protection of basic rights in Berlin's central park that had clearly distanced itself from extreme political positioning and had nothing to do with the other demonstration in front of the Reichstag. The audience of millions in front of the television only understood that the alternative thinkers were "right-wing extremists" who had attempted to storm the Reichstag. Through this staged lie the criticism against the corona measures was publicly defamed and the mood in the whole country was poisoned.

This is but one example of many, how the kernel of democracy, that is of showing respect for the other person, was radically violated. Instead of discussion there was framing and discrimination.

Lies are always a murder on the soul level; those attacked and defamed experience it as such. It is a soul abuse and violation, an attack on human dignity. To withstand this is a challenge. You need a very intact "soul-skin" in order to let it run like water off a duck's back.

Such discriminating behaviour is not new in world history. This can console us a little. I always wondered why in the Beatitudes in the Bible the need for comfort is mentioned twice. Now I understand it better – it is really necessary and I can recommend this as material for meditation.

Exercise: Meditate the Beatitudes in Matthew 5, especially the last three:

> 5:9 Blessed are the peacemakers, for they will be called children of God.

> 5:10 Blessed are those who are persecuted because of righteousness, for theirs is the kingdom of heaven.

> 5:11 Blessed are you when people insult you, persecute you and falsely say all kinds of evil against you because of me. Rejoice and be glad, because great is your reward in heaven, for in the same way they persecuted the prophets who were before you.

Strengthening your health

Exercise 14:

**Understanding illnesses, looking at
the biography of an illness**

With the corona crisis we were indoctrinated by the state
and the mainstream media with a materialistic picture of
illness. Only this counted and was taken as the guiding
principle for the coercive measures of the state. Soul and
spirit and a holistic understanding of health no longer
existed in public debate. Not even the scientific knowledge about the immune system continued to play a role.
Our governments were never concerned with strengthening the immune system and a healthy lifestyle. They
only had prohibitions and vaccinations on their sched-
ule.

It is vital to strengthen your holistic understanding
of health and to take it personally into your hands. An
illness always has underlying soul and spiritual as well
as biographical reasons that can be individual or derive
from family or society. To understand and feel this is significant for your own health.

Exercise: Remember the illnesses in your life and ask
yourself:

- What was the meaning of my illness?

- What was it like before and after?

- Were there soul or spiritual causes?

Exercise 15:

Befriend your body and its system of organs

A friendly and open attitude to our own body is one of the most vital sources of health. In fact, the body and its organs have their own soul and spirit. You can take this quite literally and can open yourself to the idea that each organ is governed by a spiritual being. You can greet and observe these organ beings while meditating. A playful approach is appropriate here.

Exercise: Imagine that each organ and part of your body is ensouled and run by elemental beings. Sit down in meditation posture and inwardly go through your organs, greeting them with a joyful smile. "Dear being of the lung, it's wonderful that you exist. I hope you are well, please receive a big smile from me." "Dear being of the liver, I greet you. What do you look like today? Let me caress you a little bit."

Be aware of the reactions; how does the feeling for your body and the mood change? Does, for instance, a joyful greeting return to you?

It is also possible that an organ being is not well. Then concern yourself with it, ask it what it needs and offer what it needs without hesitation. In the case of illness, the organ beings need special attention.

Exercise 16:

Strengthen the immune system through meditation

There are many ways to strengthen the immune system: vitamin D and C, zinc, healthy nutrition, exercise, fresh air, social contacts, singing, sufficient sleep, and so on. The following is a meditative possibility: The immune system is the physical expression of the "I", the self, that belongs to our human, spiritual nature.

Exercise: Remember your "I" in the meditation. In the pure power of attention you are close to the "I". When you feel your self as an "I", spread your "I" spiritually into all the regions of the body from head to toe, permeating your whole body with it. With this permeation by the "I", you come into close contact with the immune system and strengthen it. The immune system is also managed by many elemental beings. Thank these beings for their tireless work. For example: "Dear Immune System, dear Immune Beings, I am utterly grateful to you for taking care of me, day and night. Here I offer a song of thanks for your beneficial work."

Exercise 17:

Healing Meditation by Sigwart zu Eulenburg

There is a very beautiful meditation by Sigwart zu Eulenburg, which serves to stimulate the self-healing powers. You can use this to support any illness, and if you do it intensively and repeat it often, you can also achieve a great deal.

> Meditation for the stimulation of self-healing powers (daily in the morning and in the evening):
>
> ... Imagine the sore spot exactly as if you were approaching it from the inside, rather than from the outside. Then illuminate it so strongly that it dissolves into light before your very eyes, that is, that it almost dematerializes. At the same time, say and think through the words in a very concentrated manner:
>
> You God, who rests in me,
> On You I call! –
> Power from Your power,
> light from Your light –
> may You fill me with healing power!
>
> Through this power, may I illuminate
> all of disease's opaque matter
> and place it under the transforming rays
> of God's elemental power, working through me! –
>
> Let all darkness be filled with light,
> permeated by the purifying breath of God,
> and fulfill from now on, without ever ceasing,
> the holy law of harmony
> which, on the material plane, signifies 'health'.

(From the book *The Bridge Over the River*, Sigwart's
messages of June 30 and July 1, 1931.)

Integrating death

Exercise 18: Befriend your own death

Fear of death is a major trigger in the corona crisis. From morning to night, the media is all about avoiding death. In order to avoid death, life is shut down.

This is a futile effort, as every life ends in death. Basically, this was already clear when you were born. Nevertheless, one can observe that especially younger people do not know that one dies. They know it in theory, of course, but they have not felt it or integrated it; they secretly dream of eternal life and are then shocked when confronted with death. Here, many older people are more realistic; they have lived their lives and know that they are going to die.

What about the right to die? Who else than the individual himself, and only he or she, is entitled to determine when the moment of death should be? Raphael Bonelli, an Austrian psychotherapist, reported in a video an experience his father had, who worked as a doctor in a clinic. An almost 90 year-old man was taken to the hospital and admitted into the emergency room because of his heart problems. He became stabilized. The next day he suffered a heart attack. Mr Bonelli's father rushed to the sickroom; the old man was lying on the floor and the doctor revived him with a heart massage. Two days later, the same procedure. When the old man came slowly back to himself, he said to the doctor: "Dear doctor, can you please let me die!" The doctor backed off and finally allowed the old man to die. This caused the doctor to reflect – and should make us think, too.

The fear of death makes us unfree and manipulable. The fear of death is the entry door for a flood of irrational fears. On the other hand, an emotional preparation for your own death makes you more resilient and calms you down. Life becomes so much more intense when you reckon with death.

With every step you yourself take to reduce your fear of death, you help society relax.

Exercise: Play through your own death in a meditative manner. Suppose that you know you're going to die in a few weeks. How does that feel? Where do you want to die? How do you want to die? What do you want to get done beforehand? What burdens you, what do you definitely want to clarify before you change sides? How do you want to hand over your belongings? How should your loved ones relate to you after your passing? What are your ideas about what you will experience and do after death?

Become aware of your own little spiritual deaths

Death is less a one-off process, more an ongoing process. In a biography, you usually die several times. Change of abode, separations, strokes of fate, after which everything is different – your soul dies and is born again. Sometimes, after severe illness, the body is also reborn.

Exercise: Do you realize how many small deaths you have already died in this life? What were the causes of your deaths? How did your rebirthing take place? Who was your midwife? How did you change through this?

Exercise 20:

Respect for life dissolves the fear of death

A female friend sent me the following exciting idea: "If we respect life more and more, our fear of death will be healed. Perhaps we can all ask ourselves very deeply within and very honestly, whether we really have enough respect for life? In the very moment when I thought intensely about 'respect for life' and evoked that feeling in my heart, I found all fear of death IMMEDIATELY disappeared."

Exercise: Imagine and evoke in your heart the feeling of deepest respect and reverence for life. Then observe what happens to your fear of death.

Exercise 21:

Cultivate contact with those who have died

Our relationship with death is also so stuck, because we have lost the natural connection with those who have died. When you maintain contacts with the deceased and it becomes accepted that they live with us, inspire us, give us strength and love us, then our attitude to death changes of its own accord. The stages of the afterlife and contact with the deceased are, of course, a huge topic that cannot be dealt with here. But I would like to introduce a simple basic exercise.

Exercise: Focus yourself, enter your quiet centre within. Think of someone who has died, one that now comes to mind. Stay with this person. What feelings and impulses come up? Perhaps an inner conversation starts. Leave with a heartfelt greeting. Now think of someone else who has died, stay with that person and pay attention to the feelings and inspirations that arise. Are there any differences between the two people who have died?

Exercise 22:

What were the circumstances of my death in past incarnations?

I wondered whether to present this exercise here, as some of us might find it overwhelming. On the other hand, there are also many people who do have memories of earlier lives on earth, usually only in fragments, of course. During the course of a spiritual training and the reprocessing of one's own shadows, such memories of earlier incarnations or prenatal life surface. Today, ever more people have this as a natural gift. Of course, this is not an easy area and there are various possibilities of misinterpretation. Yet here it is not about that but about finding a more fluid relationship to death.

Exercise: Meditate the question: How many times have I actually died in past incarnations? And what were the circumstances of my death? It is not a question of precise answers, but of inklings and everything that happens inwardly in light of these questions. If you have put yourself in the position that you have already died, let's say, twenty times, and that is supported through a fine resonance in the soul, death increasingly becomes a natural process and not a one-off catastrophe.

Healing work

The following meditations presuppose the reality of the spiritual world. This is not a theory, but a real experience of those who have trained themselves for supersensory perceptions. The training of corresponding organs of perception usually requires long term practice, but there are also ever more people who bring this sensitivity from birth. With it, you are able to take a deeper look into the background of the physical world and into life as such.

In the spiritual worlds you can not only perceive, but also actively work, as long as this is supported by higher spiritual beings. Experience has proven this to be effective. The world is changing behind the scenes, letting relaxation, peace and free spaces emerge and this has a subtle and unconscious effect on everyone.

Exercise 23:

Silent declaration

The silent declaration was proposed by Marko Pogacnik:

Since public protests are forbidden in many countries, we are here to express our will in silence. Choose two to three of the proposed affirmations every day and repeat them as often as possible in silence. Speak from the bottom of your abdominal area and with the power of your heart.

Moreover, we suggest to meet together every Friday at 5:00 pm in your time zone for a silent demonstration. Imagine all of us coming together under the Tree of Life, reading the affirmations below one by one. Give each affirmation a moment of time and inner attention.

Together we are able to create better and healthier circumstances for ourselves, our children and all beings on the Earth.

1. Freedom is our birthright.

2. We demand peace on earth.

3. Democracy is our irrevocable right.

4. All efforts for a healthy earth.

5. We demand freedom of movement.

6. We respect viruses and microbes.

7. We stand for free choices.

8. We support fair and honest politicians.

9. For creative co-existence with the earth and all beings.

10. Heart-to-heart education for all children.

11. We support diversity on all levels.

12. Truthful information without any surveillance.

13. We stand for the balance of female and male properties.

The expression of hatred is not accepted. You can repeat these affirmations in the first-person, as "I", as your own inner decisions. You can pass on these suggestions, so that our silence may be heard.

Exercise 24:

Spiritually improve the sars-cov2 virus and the illness covid19

For all that exists, original living archetypes are to be found in the lower regions of the spiritual worlds called lower devachan; in the soul world (astral world) beings implement these original archetypes. This is also true for viruses and illnesses.

At the beginning of March 2020, I found in my spiritual perception of the sars-cov2 virus two special features that differentiate it from other viruses (influenza, Epstein-Barr, and so on). Firstly, it was heavily taken over by dark impulses coming from the human sphere. Secondly, it was cut off from the normal angelic hierarchies and the elemental beings of nature. At the time I wrote: "Obviously, the corona-virus is more strongly occupied by frightening adversary forces than other deadly illnesses, which, however, do not scare us as much. So, there really is much work to be done."

These two peculiarities point to the fact that the virus and the illness do not simply derive from a natural development but also from human manipulation. Interestingly enough, from the start, there was a discussion about whether the virus originated and escaped from the laboratory in Wuhan, where it was known that corona-viruses were being manipulated. In the meantime, we have plenty of external corroboration that the severity of the virus was man-made, compiled by the microbiologists Rossana Segreto (University of Innsbruck) and Prof. Roland Wiesendanger (University of Hamburg).[12] Politically, it is necessary to prohibit dangerous manipulations on viruses done in laboratories.

Spiritually, it is necessary to integrate into our evolution the sars-cov2-virus and the illness and free them from dark impulses. This was a main meditative focus for me in the spring of 2020. Fortunately enough, some good friends participated, which enormously helped

strengthen the good forces. Thus the dark impulses adhering to the spiritual virus became ever weaker, to the extent that they were no longer perceptible from June 2020 onwards. In the outer world the course of the illness became more harmless and less deadly.

However, the problem was not solved, as later dark impulses started to reappear on the spiritual virus. So, it definitely made sense to persist in working on it.

Exercise: At the start of the meditation it is advisable to connect and unite with your angel, as well as with the angelic hierarchies and Christ. All these beings secure for you a safe standpoint.

Then, with a positive attitude, meet the corona-virus beings and present Christ to them, show them the nature beings and pray for them the Lord's Prayer.

You can also approach the various aspects of these beings as a meditation on the words and observe what you perceive. For example, meditate the following words:

- Corona-virus (virus family, there are various kinds that have always been present in colds.)
- Sars-cov2 (name of the new corona-virus of the current infection wave)
- Covid19 (infectious disease through sars-cov2)

A friend of mine sent me the following, which we are happy to share with you:

"I find your approach super and the only right one – that it is our duty to attempt to integrate these viruses into earth's development. I now daily practice a redemptive meditation.

In it I think the following words:

You corona-viruses, see Christ,

see the love of Christ,

see the primordial force of love.

And see the nature beings!

Let yourself be positively integrated into the earth's
development!

For you I pray the Lord's Prayer.

Then I pray this out loud."

Exercise 25:

Create a healing space with angels and pray to free the demons of fear, manipulation and lies

Since 2020, powerful waves of fear have been running through humanity. These receive nourishment from different sources. There are fears of illness and death, existential fears due to economic shutdown and fears of a health dictatorship. These fears often rise from lower regions and befog heart and head.

In the meditative view, these fears often appear as demons, existing not only individually but collectively. There are huge demons in the astral world that overshadow entire cities and push themselves into people's souls. There are also demons that carry manipulations and lies. The hypnosis described above – spiritually seen – is carried by such demons that overshadow and displace the "I" within the soul.

Ever and again, I see that in large cities the number of such demons is far higher than in the countryside. In remote villages you feel liberated from the corona stress and regain a feeling of normality, that is, a demon-free life.

These demons permeate us and influence our soul-life. Rudolf Steiner described this as follows: "Everything you do involuntarily, everything which you feel urged to do, is caused by the activity of other beings. It does not happen out of nowhere."

And where do these demons come from? There are several sources.

Firstly, they are unconsciously produced by us humans by way of lies and false thoughts: "Beings that you yourself produce through your true or false thoughts are those that gradually grow into demons. There are good demons that derive from good thoughts. Bad thoughts, however, especially untrue ones, lies, create demonic beings of the most fearful and terrible kind, so to say, spiking through your astral-body [i.e. the soul-body]." We are talking here about enormous dimensions, as daily the worldwide number of lies and false thoughts is immeasurable.

The demons created by us humans, however, do not only remain with the one who created them, but stream into the surroundings, imprint their mood on dwellings and cities and also slip into other human beings.

A second important cause is unjust, bad laws: "All things, such as unjust, bad laws, which falsely punish people, bad institutions within social communities, all have an effect on the ether-body [i.e. the subtle or life-body of formative forces] so that in the ether-body, beings are created, which is only laughed at today in our superstitious times. These beings are spectra, ghosts." (Rudolf Steiner, Stuttgart, 7 Dec. 1907, GA 98.)

There are many unjust, bad laws and the very confusing corona prohibitions also play a part in this, resulting in masses of ghosts and demons.

Thirdly, demons are consciously produced, for example, through propaganda, intrigues and public agitation, but in addition through deliberate dark magic activities.

Unfortunately, these demons of fear, lies, deception and manipulation are systematically created on a large scale, so it is equally important to dismantle and dissolve them daily. In this regard, of course, you can easily feel overwhelmed, yet every hike starts with small steps.

In the following, I present a method that is hygienic, since you stay within yourself and your own spiritual sheaths in a protected space, so that the risk of something staying stuck in you is very slight. I am used to working together with the Christian angelic hierarchies. Those to whom this is new are invited to change or redesign the meditation as it suits them.

Exercise: I connect myself with my angel and I feel his presence. As soon as the connection is clearly there, I ask him to pass on my request to the higher angelic hierarchies to build up a healing space right in front of me. In particular, the Michaelic hosts, with their perseverance (Michael being the countenance of Christ), and the Raphaelic hosts with their healing power, form the spiritual healing space out of their sheaths. I look at this from the outside. Then I request the angelic hierarchies to bring into this healing space those demons of fear, lies and manipulation. I watch as the mood and colouring of the healing space changes. When I feel that the demons

whose turn it is for now have arrived in the healing space,
I ask the angelic hierarchies to dissolve them. I reflect
upon Christ and send His power into the healing space.
Here a pictorial depiction of Christ can be very helpful.
Finally, I send the Lord's Prayer into the healing space.
During all these steps, I remain in my position outside
the healing space. I observe whether the healing space
is changing and becoming filled with light or whether
something is still needed. If there is still something necessary, I provide it. Finally, I ask my angel to pass on my
request to the angelic hierarchies once again to dissolve
the healing space.

Exercise 26:

Bless and transform masks, tests and vaccines through prayer

Unfortunately, many of the corona measures were occupied by dark spiritual impulses. On masks and tests we found dark impulses and curses. This can lead to dislocation of the spiritual members and a weakening of the "I", or self, which brings you out of your centre and is exhausting. It seems important to me to reckon with this and not to fall blindly into it. This problem can usually be eliminated through prayer and blessing.

Vaccines not only have side effects on physical health, but they can also affect the health of soul and spirit. Rudolf Steiner clearly pointed out this serious problem. In 1917 he said that a way would be sought "… perhaps in the not-so-distant future to find a vaccine through which the organism is worked on in such a way, most likely early youth, or possibly directly from birth, that this human body cannot receive the thought that there is a soul and a spirit." (Dornach, 7 Oct. 1917, lect. 5. GA 177.) Human beings would only be able to think about the physical world and remain trapped in materialism.

The supersensory study of the new covid19 vaccines has repeatedly shown that most of them actually produce the effect of cutting off the connection to the angel, and thus to the spiritual world, and to bring into disarray the spiritual members (ether-body, astral-body, and so on). In some of the deceased after vaccination, we could observe that the effect of vaccination on the ether-body led to severe blockages in life after death. The vaccines pose a serious social problem. Individually, this can surely be resolved by medical support, spiritual work and conscious restoration of the spiritual connection, at least after some time. But what about the millions who have done damage to themselves and are not at all conscious of it? More on this issue in my book *Covid Vaccines from a Spiritual Perspective.*

Exercise: Everytime before using them, you ought to bless the various tests and medical masks in some way, for example, with the Lord's Prayer. This is usually sufficient to redeem a possible dark impulse that sits spiritually on the mask or the test. This does not seem necessary for self-sewn masks. Unfortunately, it is more complicated with the vaccines; a blessing is probably not sufficient here, but in any case it is good.

Exercise 27:

Spiritually cleanse newspaper articles, videos and films

Newspapers, videos and movies are also filled with spiritual beings. Demons of fear and manipulation are spread strongly through the media. As soon as you watch a movie, a corresponding demon slips right into your soul. This is not necessarily due to the content of the movie or article, it is more the result of the energy and spirituality with which it is charged. Often this matches the content, but this is not always the case.

Exercise: Stay vigilant when it comes to media consumption. As soon as you are negatively touched by a movie or article, stop and make a healing gesture in the direction of the movie or article. This can be a positive thought, a blessing gesture, or a prayer. Observe whether it changes your feelings.

Exercise 28:

Confront with determination the dark spirits acting in the background; take away their strength and redeem them

With the previous exercises you have a good base for spiritual self-defence. You can go spiritually deeper and meet and work together with the originary spirits behind the demons described.

The impact of the corona crisis 2020 was a profound attack on human consciousness. At the same time, it was also an opportunity, since many unredeemed burdens of the past drifted to the surface. I hope that each and every one will use their own special spiritual possibilities so that we as humanity can face this challenge.

Spiritual scientific perspective on the corona crisis

In what follows, I gather aphoristically the views that appeared most important to me regarding the spiritual understanding of the corona crisis. There are different layers of understanding that complement each other. I am unable here to enter into great detail, but if interested, please do further research. Some material for this can be found – unfortunately only in German – on our homepage:
www.anthroposophische-meditation.de/corona-krise/

Soul perspective: collective anxiety disorder

How the corona virus was dealt with publically is surprisingly similar to the structure of an anxiety disorder as described in psychology: an initial shock experience, ever more detailed protective measures through which fear is increased, zooming onto the issue, avoiding facts that play it down, etc.

Soul perspective: collective hypnosis

The mechanism of collective hypnosis was described in Exercise 9.

Astrological view: as at the beginning of the Reformation, the conjunction of Saturn and Pluto in Capricorn on Jan. 12, 2020

This special conjunction on Jan. 12, 2020 was described by astrologers as a significant beginning point of a coming time of change. For example, the astrologer Juri Viktor Stork wrote: "Saturn and Pluto were last found in conjunction in 1517, the beginning of the Reformation, when the world power of the Roman Catholic Church that had ruled for centuries was challenged and finally curtailed. It was a shockwave in the social structure, the effect of which is still felt today. The question put today is the same as then: who has the power and on what foundations does it rest? Is the demand for power still justified? Who puts up the regulations for society and who enforces them?"[13]

Today, too, we are involved in a war of beliefs. Do you believe in corona? Do you wear a mask? Do you believe in materialistic medicine? Do you have the right attitude? Who is to have power in society is a question of great pertinence. (See "The Great Reset", an initiative of the World Economic Forum (WEF), which plans a new formation of worldwide society and commerce, following the covid19 pandemic.)

Historical perspective on the 100 years since the Russian Revolution and the revival of this historical impulse

Rudolf Steiner describes a law of history, that historic impulses after 33 as well as after 100 years come to the surface more clearly.

"A human generation of 33 years ripens a seed of thought, a seed of deed. If it is ripened, it works further for 66 years in historical development. One recognizes the intensity of an impulse that human beings place into historical development, also in its effectiveness through three generations, throughout a whole century." (Rudolf Steiner, 26 Dec. 1917, in GA 180.)

What happened 100 years before the corona crisis and the worldwide lockdowns? In 1920 the Bolsheviks conquered the Mensheviks in the Russian Civil War. With this, the era of dictatorial socialism made its impression on the twentieth century. Lenin and Stalin in Russia founded their regime of compulsion. In Germany, National Socialism followed in 1933; although they fought the Communists, nevertheless a similar regime of compulsion with similar methods and aims was set up, like the Russian revolutionaries had done. After a civil war in China, Mao Zedong installed the "Republic of the People"; in many other states "social revolutions" took place.

This was always accompanied by a re-education of people and the elimination of "enemies of the state" for the Communist aim of the "ideal society". The historian Courtois estimates that in *The Black Book of Communism* the Communists have killed many people – in the Soviet Union 20 million, China 65 million, Vietnam 1 million, North Korea 2 million, Cambodia 2 million, Africa 1.7 million, Afghanistan 1.5 million, etc. Through the National Socialists approximately 25 million died. Of course, this is only the tip of the iceberg. People were brain-washed, tightly controlled and often heavily traumatized. The "anti-communist" reactions were often not much better, as for example the witch-hunt of the McCarthy era in the USA at the beginning of the Cold War.

In the reactions of governments and of society towards the corona crisis you can find a revival of these Communist impulses in history – China's extreme lockdown was praised and made into a worldwide example. State control is to dominate the life of commerce and culture. We all have to serve the higher aim of "solidarity" or "conformity", and the definition of this is given by the government. Whoever does not show solidarity, for example, meets a couple of friends, or plays football, is pursued by the police and fined heavily. Basic rights of freedom become meaningless, become subordinate to "solidarity" and "conformity". Everyone is treated equally; all are put into quarantine; it is forbidden to meet or to travel and all receive vaccination, however senseless it is. The media churns out propaganda and different opinions hardly find any voice. There are still some free spaces in social media where opinions can be voiced, but even there censorship exists. Deviants are defamed and excluded, with corresponding social and financial consequences. State control takes place worldwide, thus fitting into the aim of "world revolution". Advocates of lockdowns do not want to see through all these mists of obfuscation. This also belongs to the symptoms of communism.

The question comes up: If this is really so, how do we deal with it?

Spiritual perspective:
3 x 666 = 1998: strong influence of soratic spirits

In anthroposophy there are very differentiated descriptions of adverse spirits and fallen angels that help constitute us human beings. The "ahrimanic beings" are the spirits of materialism, cold and darkness, the "luciferic beings" are the spirits of pride, egomania and blinding light, the "asuric beings" are the spirits of fragmentation and dissolution of the "I", or self. In Sanskrit, the term "asura" means "evil spirit" or "antagonist of the gods", whereas Rudolf Steiner uses it to describe a special type of fallen angel. All these adverse spirits belong to our universe and – if they are redeemed and transformed with Christ's power, meaning the "I"-power – they can produce very positive effects. There is a fourth group that comes from spirit realms outside of our universe and actually has no place in the spirit realm of the earth, the soratic beings. These can seduce people as they promise power. Power-seeking people easily succumb to soratic beings who are the inspirers of evil. (You can find more detailed descriptions on www.anthrowiki.at.)

I would like to emphasize that this is not a theory or a belief system, but in supersensory perception one encounters these beings all the time. It is essential in a healthy spiritual schooling that one learns to deal with these beings.

Rudolf Steiner describes that in the rhythm of 666 years since the birth of Christ there has been an increased historical impact of soratic impulses. This was the spiritual background to the destruction of the Knights Templar through the Inquisition in 1312. The exact year is not important, but the time period.

3 x 666 is 1998. This is our time period. What can be discovered here?

- The above-mentioned inhuman dictatorships of the 20th century were gigantic "landing grounds" of soratic beings. We are all still in the midst of these issues.

- At the end of the 20th century, new technologies were introduced, digitization, mobile phone technology and genetic engineering. These techniques shape people deeply and can have a destructive effect on the soul and on consciousness. These technologies are also large landing grounds for soratic beings; supersensory research has confirmed this over the past few decades. Highly sensitive people feel this and often react very strongly, for instance, to cell phone radiation, not because of the physical radiation, but because they experience the soratic effects riding on it.

Spiritual Perspective on the imminent incarnation of Ahriman

I know the phrase "imminent incarnation of Ahriman" is difficult for someone who is not deeply acquainted with anthroposophy. To understand it you need basic knowledge that first needs to be worked through. With that in mind, please read on with open-mindedness.

In 1909 Rudolf Steiner spoke of the danger of an "intolerable tyranny" due to political abuse of the fear of germs: "It seems that what is one of the greatest goods of human life [health] is at the mercy of political parties. [...] What, for example, would mankind be faced with, when the fear of germs [viruses] is exploited and provisions of a legal nature against the control of germs [or viruses] are created? [...] It would become an impossible situation, an intolerable one leading to tyranny" (Rudolf Steiner, Munich, 6 March 1909, source: steinerdatabase.de).

In 1919, in several lectures, Rudolf Steiner described that the incarnation of Ahriman was due at the beginning of the third millennium. Reading his descriptions really puts you in the present day. Rudolf Steiner shows some currents that are preparing the incarnation of Ahriman. They include scientific materialism, an intellectual life driven by the economy, the preservation of knowledge in libraries and today on electronic data carriers, the belief in the omnipotence of numbers and statistics, the emphasis on party antagonisms, the establishment of a world government, and so on.

The incarnation of Ahriman must be thought of as a lengthy process. The ahrimanic spirits sink step by step into the different realms of the human being. When Ahriman penetrates the "I", the self, one no longer experiences it, one is absorbed by the outside world. This has been the case for centuries. One can overcome this work of Ahriman through meditation, religion, art or intensive thinking. When ahrimanic beings veil thinking, one receives abstract, lifeless thoughts. This is regarded by many as the standard today for, to a large extent, the ahrimanic beings have already occupied the space of thinking. In the present time the ahrimanic beings are especially fighting for power over the realm of people's feelings; the more the incarnation of Ahriman progresses into the realm of feelings, the more impoverished or less capable of feeling you become. But also the ahrimanization of human life-bodies has begun. The result already visible today is the machine man with artificial intelligence, the ideal of transhumanism.

The incarnation of Ahriman is an event necessary in human evolution. But this can take place in different ways. It is possible that we human beings learn how to deal with it, absorb and process the ahrimanic impulses

without losing the "I", the soul and spiritual connection. Through this, the ahrimanic beings would also be redeemed. But there is also another possibility, that we human beings lose our humanity and become machines. This is all the more the case when the incarnation of Ahriman is used by soratic beings and consequently takes place prematurely. With the current soratic culmination, this seems to be the case. Rudolf Steiner foresaw this. His descriptions of Ahriman's incarnation and the establishment of a political world dictatorship, the disruption of one's own independent thinking and the introduction of vaccinations in order to destroy our connection to the spiritual world, correspond to this possibility.

Spiritual Perspective on the proselytizing of materialism and transhumanism

The amazing events since January 2020 in the corona crisis make sense when viewed from the perspective of a modern religious war. With religious zeal, the new materialistic world religion carried out a worldwide forced mission. The worshipped gods are the soratic-ahrimanic spirits. However, this is cleverly concealed and not recognizable at first glance. This religion appears as "self-evident truth" and is not organized as a formal religious community. An ideological spearhead is transhumanism, in which the goal of the transition from man to machine is formulated.

This dimension suddenly became apparent to me when in 2020 the dead no longer received last rites and even Easter was cancelled; there were no services and instead on Easter Sunday, the most important Christian holiday, the day of redemption, the day of Christ's resurrection, Bill Gates gave a long prime-time TV interview and said that all seven billion people would now be vaccinated and thus saved. In religious wars, old holidays are occupied and filled with new content. Bill Gates acted like a prophet of a new religion without even realizing it.

The unspoken creed of the materialistic world religion is something like this:

- There is no spiritual world, only the material world. (This is precisely the inspiration of Ahrimanic spirits, who claim not to be spirits.)
- Sickness is the devil, dying is hell. Both must be avoided.

- Our heaven is survival. We want eternal life on earth.

- Our redeemer and saviour is technical medicine and vaccines.

- Since we only consist of matter, our bodies can be replaced by technology.

- We receive eternal life if our brain is replaced by a computer (what transhumanists are actually working on today).

- Other people are dangerous virus spreaders; fear your neighbour.

- Our religious rituals are social distancing and masking.

- Nature is annoying and exhausting. We don't want to be dependent on her any longer. We no longer want to look at nature, but at screens. We will build test-tube cities and food is also to be produced in the test-tube.

- Science must only serve our gods.

- The other religions are allowed to continue superficially if they serve our gods at their core.

- We don't tell anyone that this is a religion, so that nobody gets the idea that one could turn away from it and connect with other gods.

What can we do?

We have been faced with this question "What's to be done?" for decades, but with the corona crisis it became very urgent. I see two main answers:

Firstly, it is important to persevere, to remain connected to the real spiritual world, even if it is lost to much of humanity. This must be carried through, come what may, so that those not on board at present have the chance to reconnect in the future once the necessary learning processes have been completed. It is about spiritual resilience and as a result, of course, also about social resilience. All the exercises described in this little book are given for this purpose.

Secondly, it is important, by means of spiritual healing, to free and redeem the ahrimanic spirits from the soratic influence. This is possible because Christ, Michaelic spirits and many other spirits can handle it well and are ready for it. Going deeper here is a task for specialists, one should not burden oneself with it unless one feels called. But through prayer and spiritual work, everyone can help.

Rudolf Steiner on fear and the power of healing

"In our time, as we know, there is a fear that is similar to the fear in the Middle Ages regarding ghosts. Today this is the fear of germs [viruses]. The two conditions of fear are objectively completely the same. They are also the same in so far as each of the two ages, the Middle Ages and modern times, behave in a way appropriate to them. The Middle Ages had a certain belief in the spiritual world and therefore, of course, a fear of spiritual beings. The modern age has lost this belief in the spiritual world. It believes in matter; it is consequently afraid of material beings, however small they might be [...]

Now, the most essential point today, is that germs [viruses] can only become dangerous when they are nurtured [...] Germs [viruses] are nurtured most intensively when the human being takes into his sleep nothing else but a materialistic attitude [...] There is at least one more means of nurturing germs, which is as good as the one I mentioned, and that is to live in a cluster of epidemic illnesses and to absorb nothing else but the pictures of the illnesses surrounding one, in that one is solely filled with the feeling of fear of these illnesses [...] If one is not able to bring forth anything else than the fear of these illnesses (which occur all around one in an epidemic hot-spot of illness) and one goes to sleep at night with the thought of fear, then in the soul unconscious after-images, imaginations penetrated by fear are produced. And this is a good means to nurture germs [viruses]. If one is able, only a little, to reduce this fear through actions filled with love, for example, in caring for the sick, and one can forget that one might also get infected, then the nurturing forces for the germs [viruses] become weaker [...].

One could work in a much more satisfying way for the future of humanity, if one gave people imaginations through which they became less materialistic and were empowered by the spirit to bring love into their deeds. One has to get used to the idea that what one regards as a direct healing force through spiritual science has to work through the human community."

(Rudolf Steiner, Basel, 5 May 1914, GA 154.)

"If courage is not to sink ..."

"We must eradicate from the soul, root and branch, the fear and horror of what is coming upon mankind in the future.

Man must acquire composure in relation to all feelings and sensations regarding the future. Face everything that may come with absolute equanimity, and only think that whatever may come our way comes through the wisdom-filled guiding forces of the world. We have to do what is right at the moment and leave everything else to the future.

Part of what we have to learn in this time is to live out of pure trust, without any security for our existence, out of trust in the ever-present help from the spiritual world. Truly, there is no other way today if courage is not to sink. Let us discipline our will and seek awakening from within, every morning and every evening."

(Rudolf Steiner, Bremen, November 27, 1910.)

Endnotes:

1)   https://www.preprints.org/manuscript/202010.0330/v2

https://macdonaldlaurier.ca/files/pdf/20201209_Rethinking_lockdowns_Joffe_COMMENTARY_FWeb.pdf

(2)   E.g. Angela Merkel: https://www.focus.de/politik/deutschland/corona-schock-fuer-kanzlerin-merkel-raeumt-in-interner-schalte-ein-uns-ist-das-ding-entglitten_id_12909341.html)

(3)   https://tkp.at/2021/01/11/stanford-studie-mit-top-medizin-wissenschaftler-ioannidis-zeigt-keinen-nutzen-von-lockdowns/?fbclid=IwAR0vb0LE3LnM1iYJ_Obh57M8IlowBg_3BMyvERDdTRAH9hIbvaBdebTOU_8)

(4)   https://reitschuster.de/post/merkel-harter-corona-kurs-ist-politische-entscheidung/

(5)   https://www.destatis.de/DE/Themen/Gesellschaft-Umwelt/Bevoelkerung/Sterbefaelle-Lebenserwartung/_inhalt.html

(6)   https://www.rki.de/DE/Content/InfAZ/N/Neuartiges_Coronavirus/Situationsberichte/Jan_2021/2021-01-02-de.pdf?__blob=publicationFile

(7)   https://www.rki.de/DE/Content/InfAZ/N/Neuartiges_Coronavirus/Situationsberichte/Jan_2021/2021-01-19-de.pdf?__blob=publicationFile

(8)   https://tkp.at/2021/01/17/keine-beweise-fuer-ansteckung-durch-asymptomatische-personen/

https://tkp.at/2020/12/21/gibt-es-beweise-fuer-asymptomatische-ansteckung/

https://tkp.at/2020/10/27/coronavirus-so-ansteckend-sind-asymptomatisch-infizierte/

https://tkp.at/2020/08/20/asymptomatische-uebertragung-gibt-es-das-studien/

https://sciencefiles.org/2020/12/28/explosive-studie-asymptomatische-falle-nicht-ansteckend-kein-grund-fur-lockdowns/?highlight=asymptomatisch

https://sciencefiles.org/2020/12/22/vorsatzlich-sittenwid-rig-geschadet-christian-drosten-mit-einem-bein-vor-geri-cht/?highlight=asymptomatisch

https://sciencefiles.org/2020/12/28/das-asymptomatische-sars-karten-haus-sturzt-ein-nachste-studie-findet-kaum-asymptoma-tische-ubertragung/?highlight=asymptomatisch

https://corona-transition.org/symptomlose-seien-nun-die-treib-er-der-pandemie-die-who-widerspricht

https://corona-transition.org/who-corona-infizierte-ohne-symp-tome-sind-keine-ubertrager

(9) https://tkp.at/2021/02/15/propaganda-der-regierung-zu-ge-faehrlichen-mutationen-wahr-oder-unwahr/

https://tkp.at/2021/02/14/epidemiologe-virus-variant-en-machen-nicht-mehr-krank/

https://tkp.at/2021/02/12/varianten-in-suedafrika-und-eng-land-haben-rueckgang-nicht-aufhalten-koennen/

(10) https://www.kekstcnc.com/media/2793/kekstcnc_research_covid-19_opinion_tracker_wave-4.pdf?fbclid=IwAR0hM-cddEZUPlCYBWNPRwSlCf8SaZ32RPFkW_Bzuz5qmiLG-2TZUP88L6N5A

https://www.spiegel.de/psychologie/die-angst-vor-corona-ist-groesser-als-das-tatsaechliche-risiko-a-80c1a0c8-c5c3-46f2-ba45-22a6270e1db8

(11) https://wiki.sonnenstaatland.com/wiki/R%C3%BCdiger_Hoff-mann?fbclid=IwAR13z6obkZvznaWldQ73i3HLqzoyktEqFt_XLQXXuuVDOU4wPjA49RcUlWs#Sturm_auf_den_Reichstag_und_andere_Veranstaltungen

(12) https://www.heise.de/tp/features/Kommt-Sars-CoV-2-aus-dem-Labor-5030073.html

https://www.researchgate.net/publication/349302406_Studie_zum_Ursprung_der_Coronavirus-Pandemie

(13) https://spuren.ch/content/single-ansicht-news/datum////tanz-auf-der-schwelle.html

Thomas Mayer

Answering the Call of the Elementals

**Practices for Connecting with Nature Spirits
A Passionate Plea for Help**

We all live in the realm of elemental beings. They permeate our souls, our thoughts, our feelings, and they co-create the world around us, yet we are often completely unaware of them. They, however, are eager to be perceived and acknowledged by us because their future and ours are fundamentally connected.

Elementals act as carriers of the emotional level of the world, and Thomas Mayer reveals how he learned to develop and fine-tune his faculty of perception in order to make direct personal contact with them. Providing insight into the elemental hierarchy, from the lowly workers to the masters and the elemental kings, he portrays Christ elemental beings, social elementals, and even machine elementals. He also explores adversary forces such as Lucifer and Ahriman that access the elemental world through the human subconscious and seek to destroy our elemental friends.

Through sharing his encounters with fairies, dwarves, giants, and others, the author reveals their urgent call for help, an entreaty to anchor the elemental beings again in the awareness of humankind through recognition, acknowledgment, and conscious connection. Let us support the elementals in their crucial, life-giving work, through which they in turn support us in preserving the Earth we live on.

Pages: 160, $16.99
ISBN: 9781644112144
Publisher: Findhorn Press

Answering the Call
of the Elementals
Practices for Connecting
with Nature Spirits
Thomas Mayer

Thomas Mayer

Covid Vaccines from a Spiritual Perspective

Consequences for the Soul and Spirit and for Life after Death

Vaccination is a topic that has long divided opinion. Today, in view of Covid-19, that debate has become ever more polarized.

Illustrated throughout with full-colour images, *Covid Vaccines from a Spiritual Perspective* deals with scientific facts, but also with research that requires spiritual-scientific methods. Led by main author and activist Thomas Mayer, the volume features reports, experiences and commentary from more than fifty contributors with clairvoyant and psychic abilities. From their observations, it is argued that Covid vaccines are not 'harmless jabs', but potentially violent interventions in the subtle structures of the human body, soul and spirit. The vaccines even have implications for an individual's life beyond death. Instead of the soul evolving in the afterlife, it could remain bound to the earth and suffer deeply.

Although this book's conclusions may appear alarming, it is not the author's intention to create fear. He seeks only to provide useful information and enlightenment, demonstrating how vaccinated and unvaccinated people can deal with this subject consciously, courageously and with hope for the future.

Pages: 392, £25.99
ISBN: 978 3 910465 00 8

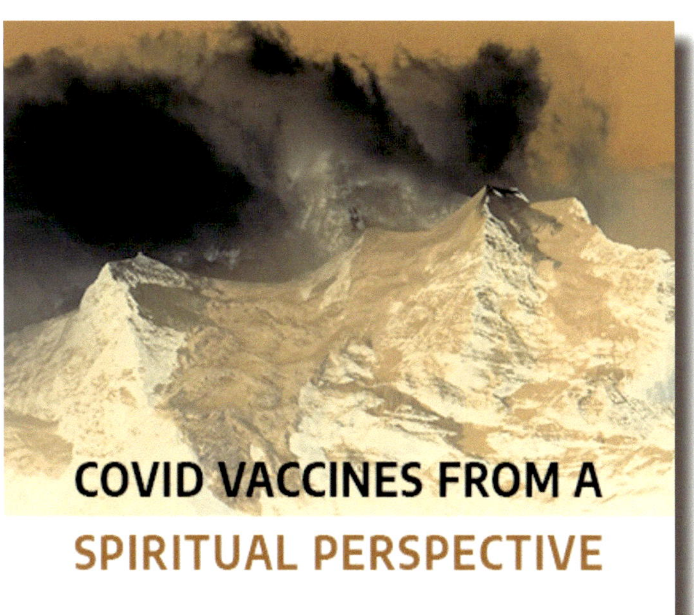

COVID VACCINES FROM A
SPIRITUAL PERSPECTIVE

Consequences for the Soul and Spirit and for Life after Death

Thomas Mayer

About the author:

Thomas Mayer

Meditation teacher, author, civil rights activist

Thomas Mayer was born in southern Germany. He is co-founder of "More Democracy", an association in Germany to further direct democracy or participatory politics, particularly through referenda. He has organized many local referenda. He has lectured widely on the subject of regional currencies and initiated pilot projects to introduce these. He organized a referendum in Switzerland called "sovereign money" that was voted on in 2018 regarding the question of who should have the right to create money, private banks or public institutions. Since 2004 he has been teaching Anthroposophical Meditation together with Agnes Hardorp.

Book Publications:
- *Triumph der Bürger! Mehr Demokratie in Bayern*, 1997
- *Kunstwerk Volksabstimmung*, 2004
- *Erlebnis Erdwandlung*, 2008
- *Rettet die Elementarwesen*, 2008
- *Zusammenarbeit mit Elementarwesen, Gespräche mit Praktikern*, 2010
- *Zusammenarbeit mit Elementarwesen 2, Neue Interviews mit Forschern und Praktikern*, 2012
- *Vollgeld, Das Geldsystem der Zukunft*, 2014
- *Wie Banken Geld aus Nichts erzeugen*, 2018
- *Spirituelle Notwehr in der Coronakrise - 28 Meditationen*, 2021
- *Corona-Impfungen aus spiritueller Sicht*, 2021
- *Ratgeber Impfdruck und Impfpflicht*, 2022

Websites:

www.anthroposophical-meditation.info

www.thomasmayer.org